OMG! 10 Super Simple Steps for Career Success

Essentials for Job Seekers and Staff Members

By Tish Times

Why you should read this book:

OMG! 10 Super Simple Steps for Career Success

is the book for you if:

- You want to know how to transition from a job you HATE so you can embark on a career you LOVE, enjoy your work and earn what you are worth.

- You think that some of your PAST errors are hindering you from having a successful NOW.

- You have tried the 'traditional job search methods' but have not yet landed your IDEAL gig.

- You have ever BOMBED an interview and are not sure what you could have done to be better prepared.

This book is the best beginning to unlocking your AMAZING!

For more information visit www.tishtimes.com

This book is dedicated to my family
My Husband: Roy Edward Times, My Sons: Derrell Peoples,
Lavell Jones, and Charles Times
And...little Aaliyah Jones (my 1st Grandbaby)
I love you more than you may ever understand. Thank you for
always believing in me. Roy – Your gentle nudge was what I
needed to move into what once seemed impossible. – I love you.

To Dr. Mikel Brown – Who, among many other things, helped
me negotiate salary for my first real job in the employment
industry over 15 years ago...I appreciate your voice, leadership
and guidance.

Lillie Peoples, Cassandra Pelham, Teddy Pelham, Rodney
Peoples, Terri Peoples,
L.T. Peoples, Jr. & Terry Peoples, Mary "LizFoxx" Campbell,
LaTascha Durden, Belinda Johnson, Charles Newman, my God
children and all of my friends and clients – Thank you for your
prayers and support.

Thank You to my Editor – Caryn C. Newman (Cay-Ren) ☺

And.... To every job seeker and career professional who is
searching for that dream job – let these steps begin the journey
towards the fruition of your dream!

Cover photography by: LaTascha Durden Photography
Cover by: Dominic Patridge of **Ground Zero Management**

Contents

Appendix Bonuses!
- **Tips for Creating a Great Resume**
- **Basic Social Media Tips for Job Search**
- **Creating Work/Life Balance**
- **Transitioning into Your New Job!**

What folks are saying about Tish Times:

Erin Flores Ritter - Legislative Aide at City of El Paso, Texas

Tish is a dynamic person who exhibits her passion and commitment to matching people with the right career. Through personal interaction and networking events, Tish provides a much needed service to both job seekers and companies looking for the right people. Tish helps her clients see new opportunities or possibilities they may not have discovered on their own.

Benita Munoz - Relationship Manager at ADP

I have had the pleasure of working directly and indirectly with Tish for 10+ years. As an entrepreneur, her knowledge of business is just outstanding. Tish demonstrates a passion for what she does and has a real talent for business. She is truly an expert in the field of recruitment and career coaching and I trust what she has to say. Over the years, the quality of the individuals that Tish has referred to me has always been top notch. In addition, I have benefited from her coaching skills by receiving solid advice, direction and recommendations – both personal and professional. Because of my participation in the events sponsored by HireTimes Career & Coaching Group, I have had fun increasing my business network, meeting outstanding potential candidates, and increasing my knowledge and skills in the various topics presented by her panel of experts! Without a doubt, Tish receives my highest recommendation!

Maria Ibarra – Office Manager, Hear on Earth

I have seen Tish Times help multiple people through her career coaching services and networking events. When I was in need of a career change Tish was up to the challenge. Through her network and ability to see the perfect opportunity for her clients, she connected me with my current employer. When I was apprehensive about my ability to fulfill the job responsibilities, Tish coached me, identified my hidden strengths and brought them to the surface. She helped to prepare me for the interview that secured my new career. I am now working in an environment that I love and that is ideal for me. I would recommend Tish Times to any person looking to improve their career opportunities.

FORWARD by
Mark Victor Hansen co-author of Chicken Soup for the Soul

Work is a basic human right. In fact a basic human need! We each need to contribute to feel complete and grow our self-esteem and self-respect.

Continued herein are 10 super simple steps to work towards the career of your heart's desire, right livelihood and passion. To live fully, fulfilling your destiny.

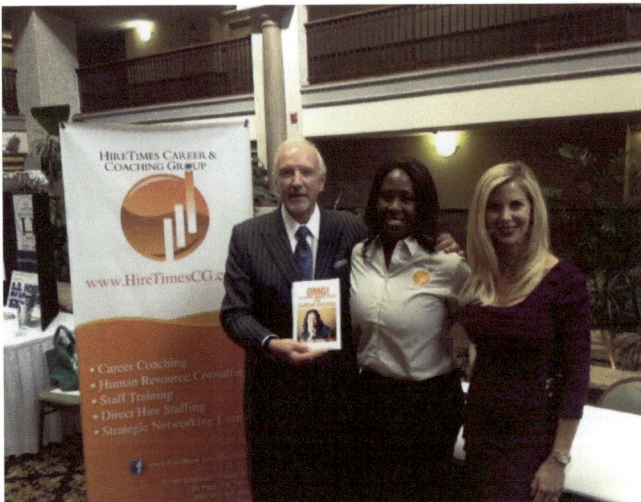

OMG! 10 Super Simple Steps for Career Success
Essentials for Job Seekers and Staff Members
Tish Times

Something has to change. Many years ago, I tried to stop the obsession I have with the world of employment. I became so sick of seeing employees who cannot bear to get up on Monday morning to put in one more hour at a job that they hate. I found myself even more repulsed by thinking about all of the job seekers who were trying, as hard as they knew how, to find that "ideal" position to no avail. After entering the staffing industry in the early nineties and working for 6 years as a Staffing Coordinator, I took a brief hiatus. I was tired of sending an eager job candidate to a temporary position, seeing them obtain the job, only to return to my office 6 months later and start the process all over. There was too much pressure in finding hundreds of employees for large manufacturing companies on strict deadlines. I told myself I was burned out.

I thought I would be a fitness trainer, a non-profit manager or something different. Well...none of those worked out and my obsession to help people find their ideal career path still dominated my thoughts. I knew there had to be a way to help people jump start their job search with the tools to secure full time employment, that wasn't just another "gig", but instead, an ideal career move that was based on their passions and strengths. Something they could truly enjoy and earn an excellent salary.

I came to realize, sometimes their path may include starting their own business opposed to finding traditional employment, but nonetheless they could find something they love.

It was from all of this that I gave birth to my company, "HireTimes Career & Coaching Group", which now helps prepare job seekers, the underemployed, and others stuck in dead end jobs; figure out a career path and a way to go get it! These are some Super Simple Steps that you MUST KNOW to navigate the ins and outs of your job search and ultimate career success. (Remember, this is my magnificent obsession and I want you to benefit from my years of guiding people to their optimal careers!)

Step 1: Know Who You Are

Labels. The most important thing to remember is that the most powerful 'label maker' lives in your head. It is that voice that always tries to remind you of how you screwed up your last position or how your scale read three pounds heavier last week. If you are not sure of who you are, "folks" will label you with words that describe your past, your appearance, your family, or your physical location. Those secure in themselves are fully aware that these things do not define them. All of your past failures do not fully make up the person you are today. Some of the negative things that happen in your life often drown out the greatness that you once knew to be true about yourself. ***Knowing who you are is the prerequisite for authenticity***. Every employment expert would agree that you should dress appropriately for an interview, but here is a different spin on what you may have heard before. Take your own personal style – then dress it up. Showing up to an interview in a tailored suit, hair slicked up into a bun and wearing sensible shoes may sound like the right thing for a woman to do. If in fact you would, on a normal day, wear a retro outfit with platform shoes, why not take your own authentic style and upgrade it to be a more professional version of yourself? It is quite common to draw your idea of professionalism from magazines and television and become a carbon copy of what seems professional.

However, if you are creating a false image that causes you to veer substantially from the person you really are, you are being inauthentic. Although wearing Hollywood's version of professional is a great choice for some, if it is not authentically you, it will become difficult for you to maintain the façade over time. If after a few weeks, you become more comfortable in your role, and begin to arrive to work in attire that is more suited to your personality, it could make you look fraudulent. At least when a hiring manager sees a true depiction of who you are during the interview (still professional and interview appropriate) they know what they are getting and will not get a rude awakening when 'the real you' shows up. Knowing who you are gives you the ability to work in a setting that best fits your skill set, disposition, and comfort level. One of my favorite shows is Undercover Boss. An episode just aired which featured a retail surf shop. The CEO made mention of the fact that his father was a physician, and that he had been groomed to follow in his father's footsteps. The CEO, however, desired to work in an atmosphere that allowed him to dress more casually and have a more laid back approach to work. Therefore, he chose to work for a company that makes and sells sporting attire. On the show, this CEO whizzed down the hall on a skateboard decked out in khakis and a t-shirt on the way to his executive office. Everyone in the company is committed to sporting their casual, active wear and the company is very successful. If working in this type of climate seems appealing to you, do not allow yourself to be talked into a three-piece suit, working in an office on the 50th floor, only to be miserable everyday as you ride up the elevator to your corporate career. ***Know you and BE YOU!*** You can succeed in doing what you want on your terms if you are willing to do what it takes to make it happen. ***Knowing who you are creates the liberty to set boundaries in the workplace, enabling you to work in an environment that is safe and productive.*** As a professional who spent many years in the corporate world, I did not find myself in the midst of workplace drama. The things that I have been sure about for many years are:

I AM honest. I AM not a gossip. I AM a hard worker. I AM a woman with a strong work ethic. I AM passionate about the work that I do.

Being sure of self makes it easy to decide what I will and will not do. I have never had to announce these characteristics to my new co-workers. Rather, I modeled the level of respect and professionalism that I wanted given to me. If you maintain a standard for yourself at work, others will have no choice but to uphold it. When you are conducting your job search do not allow the pressure of being unemployed to cause you to deviate from the person you are deep inside. If you truly want to work in a certain profession and are qualified to do so, let nothing stop you from reaching your goal.

Even if you must bridge your financial needs with a temporary position, if it is not your ultimate passion, keep your eyes and heart focused on what you really want. Consider the lion. If he found himself in a fight last week with a powerful adversary that gave him the fight of his life, even if he barely escaped, you would not see him today with a saunter that is sluggish. The lion's head would not be downcast. In fact, if you were in his line of vision, you would likely become his decadent feast for the day! The lion innately exhibits strength. At no time does a lion allow his past defeats to dictate his future victories. He knows who he is. Do you? Remember – who you are is not predicated on how you feel at the moment, but who you know in your heart that you were created to be.

Right now:

Turn to the appendix in the back of this book and write down five things about yourself that are amazing.

Write ten **"I AM" statements** that really speak to you. Write each one in the present tense. Read these statements aloud each morning.

Examples: I AM Confident, I AM Healthy, I AM a Good Employee, I AM the next CEO, etc.

Step 2: **Know What You Want**

Knowing what you want is a natural progression from knowing who you are. Have you heard the term 'fuzzy goals'? If you ask your boss for a raise but you are not clear exactly how much of a pay increase you desire, you should not be disappointed if you receive a dime more per paycheck. When you are not clear with your requests, you cannot expect to receive your true desires. Many of us were taught this ideal as children. When we would visit family friends I remember my mother saying things such as, "don't you ask for anything when we get there" or "don't be greedy, don't ask for seconds – even if they offer"!

I know my mother was trying to teach me lessons in being polite, however do you realize that these instructions can also negatively influence us when we enter romantic relationships, or join the workforce? I coach people all the time who are afraid to ask for what they really want. Instead, they settle for what is offered to them. As a recruiter I have seen many hiring managers who were prepared to make a high salary offer, however when the candidate was asked their salary requirements they sufficed to accept the entry level salary instead of making a professional demand for a salary commiserate with their experience and expertise.

What type of job search plan do you have in place? Whether you currently have a job or not, there should be some thought behind the way you apply for jobs. If you open a well-known job search engine every morning and apply for every new listed job opening, the likelihood of you being hired anytime soon is very low. I am not saying that it has not worked for some people, but the percentage is extremely small. Develop a method to your search. Get more creative.

Research a different way to do a job search that will differentiate you from the thousands of applicants who are applying for the same job you are. I have only had three traditionally professional (my high school and college fast food gigs do not count) jobs prior to going into business for myself; none of which were secured through a traditional job search method. I know it is possible – get out of your head and do something different.

When making a career shift, figure out exactly what you want to do, where you want to do it, and with whom you would like to do it. I love to use the example of a client who wanted to be an attorney; however, she had not completed her degree. She believed that she could find employment that valued her professionalism but also would welcome her quirky personality and unique style. She researched the law firms in her area. In her searching, she found one firm that was very successful, but not as "stuffy" as a traditional law office. She wanted to work in a mentoring environment where lawyers were hard working and professional, but also laid back and caring.

She went through the traditional application process to apply as an Administrative Assistant, thinking she could get her foot in the door while she completed her education. This applicant delivered a hand written card thanking the partners for interviewing her. Determined to be a part of this unique office environment, she then followed up with a letter inquiring about the status of the position when she had not gotten a call within two weeks. The result was a phone call inviting her to join the team, for which she of course, was overjoyed. I believe it was evident to the hiring team at that law firm that she was not only qualified to work there, but that her strong desire to be a part of their staff would also fuel her productivity. They were correct, she worked her way through law school and now works there as an attorney.

Conversely, I recently coached a client who has the most bubbly, welcoming disposition you could imagine. She was quite noticeably a front office, face-to-face type of employee who excels in a customer service or sales environment. Her boss hired me to coach her, due to a lack of productivity on her part. The moment I met her I knew that she was in the wrong job for her personality type. Her role was in a back office, working alone, facing a computer screen all day. She was miserable and her work was substandard. When I asked her why she accepted the position she responded with a familiar answer, "I needed a job and I took the first thing I could find". Her stint with that company lasted for less than a year and she has since moved into a position in which she can really use her experience and education *and* the job is a better match for her personality.

Do not confuse what you want for what you need! It would be more advantageous to accept a temporary position that you know is just a short-term engagement, until you find what you really want to do. Whatever you do, do not give up on WHAT YOU WANT!

Step 3: **Prep like a Mad Man**

I will never forget the well-dressed, well-groomed, professional MBA who came into my office to apply for a position with my company. She looked the part, she was articulate, and I was hopeful that I had found "the one". I then asked the one question I ask every applicant - "What do you know about my organization"? She stared at me, eyes glazed over and began to recite how she had planned to do the research but did not have time and blah, blah, blah. Most hiring managers want to interview a candidate who has done some homework concerning their company. It shows a genuine interest and gives a sneak peek into the level of commitment they will make to the company should they be hired. Take the time, do the research. With technology literally at our fingertips, there is no excuse for not knowing about the company you have been selected to interview for. With the advent of social networking, you can dig several layers into an organization and learn about individual members of the company via their Linked-In profile, as well as other social media sites.

Practice talking about YOU!

You would be surprised how many people do not know how to elaborate on their resume! Study your resume. Remember your timeline; length of time at each position, and be able to explain any gaps with confidence. This is especially important if you have a professional resume writer to construct your resume. Make sure that it resonates with you and that you can easily expound on it if necessary. If there are any negatives, such as terminations, short time stints, or legal issues, you should be ready to hold your head high and describe the circumstances.

Be prepared to discuss what you have learned from any negative experiences that have prepared you to be an asset to the organization, to which you are applying. Drill yourself (or have someone help you). Practice answering any possible question that may arise. Get comfortable with your answers; make them real. You do not want to sound like a robot nor do you want to come off insincere. **Do the work!** – It can make all the difference in your career.

Also, be prepared to answer the dreaded question/the request that trips up so many. This should be the easiest part of the interview, however so many fail to excel at the request to -*"Tell me about yourself"*. This is why **number one** on the Super Simple Steps list is so vital. Most interviewees will begin to describe what they have done, not who they are. If I want to know what you have done, I can read your application. If I ask you to tell me about yourself, I want to know what type of work ethic you possess. What type of character do you bring? Are you loyal, hardworking, and committed?

Think these things through and be prepared to WOW the interviewer with your answers.

Use your Google! Look up potential interview questions for the industry that you are seeking to work. You will find hundreds of possible questions. You do not have to memorize each one, but practice several answers for a few dozen of the questions. Although you cannot anticipate exactly what questions they may ask, you will be much better prepared than the average Joe who has not done any prep work!

Do the prep work for the interview, but know when to **SHUT UP!** One of the worst things a job seeker can do during an interview is babble. When a question is asked, be sure to answer the question asked of you. Whatever you do, however, do not allow your nerves to cause you to ramble on and on about things that may be related to the interview, but cause you to seem incapable of succinctly articulating a thought. Practice focusing on one thought at a time. It is a huge turn off for an interviewer to have to keep refocusing you back to the question at hand. You may not even realize that you lose focus or ramble; I encourage you to speak to a trusted friend and ask their honest opinion. If that is not feasible, schedule a mock interview with a local career center and ask them to provide you with feedback. If you are guilty of being a 'rambler', hire a career coach to assist you in developing your interviewing skills. Having good professional guidance will prove invaluable for your job search.

Step 4: Be Confident

The best way for me to describe the importance of confidence is to tell you a personal story. This importance goes hand-in-hand with knowing who you are and knowing what you want. As a young adult, I was a victim of domestic violence (first marriage – not with my current FABULOUS husband of 17 years as of 2013). In high school, I was the captain of my varsity basketball team, a student council member, voted as part of the prom court, and I made very good grades. I had the appearance of a very confident person. Unfortunately, that façade of confidence came from all of the exterior accolades that I received due to charisma and athleticism.

I had no concept of self-worth or true confidence. That was evidenced by the fact that I married the first guy who showed me any real attention and told me that he loved me. What does all of this have to do with confidence for career success? EVERYTHING! It was not until I learned to love myself completely that I began to exude true confidence. Once I realized that I was put on this earth for more than to be some guy's punching bag, that I was beautiful inside and out, and that I was smart and had a lot to offer, I began to see myself differently.

The person I was, prior to the transformation, at work (as well as everywhere else) is so vastly different from the person I am now. It is literally like two different people. Unlike the previous version of myself a few years earlier, when I applied for my last positions in the traditional workforce and went on an interview I knew beyond any doubt that I was the best candidate for the job. I knew how to convey that to the interviewer and was able to secure the jobs for which I interviewed. It was not conceit or cockiness; I was self-assured.

What does it take to have the type of confidence that makes a hiring manager or decision maker believe that you are just the person for the job? First, you must understand that confidence does not start on the outside. Confidence does not come from size, physical appearance, or clothing. If that were the case, you would not meet that occasional overweight person who knows who he or she is and emanates poise regardless of their size. Confidence does not stem from how you feel. If you ask many public speakers, they will admit that they still get nervous every time they stand before an audience. The anxiety they experience, however, does not detract from their sureness.

Optimism is important for developing a strong sense of self. You have to believe that God put you on earth to make a difference. Surround yourself with people who are confident, even more so than yourself. Never be afraid to have strong people in your life who possess characteristics that you admire. You will rise or fall to the level of those closest to you. Most important, remind yourself of who you are. Read scripture, speak affirmations that confirm your confidence, rehearse your "I AM" statements. Never allow how you feel to dictate what you believe; believe that you are amazing and allow that belief to drive how you see yourself.

Step 5: Focus on Your Strengths

I love to tell the story about my earlobe. Most people do not even notice, but my son Lavell, when he was about two years old, grabbed my hoop earring and pulled it while we were playing. His goal was not to cause me tremendous pain; he was just a baby. When he pulled it, the earring ripped my earlobe. I already had three pierces in my earlobe, so now I just wear an earring in the next closest hole.

I do lots of public speaking and training. At no time have I opened a seminar by saying, "I know I might look well put together, but please focus your attention on my torn earlobe." I assure you, many of my friends and associates reading this now are saying, "Really? I never knew she had a torn earlobe!" Just as I do not focus on or bring attention to what might be considered a flaw, neither should you continuously focus on your weaknesses. When preparing for an interview, talk about things in which you excel. Many cultures teach humility, but almost to a fault. I spoke with a client about her sterling reputation in her field and tried to get her to expound on her experience. She said that it made her uncomfortable to talk about herself. An interview situation is not the time to be shy about your strong points. There is nothing humble about shrinking back for fear of sounding arrogant! TOOT YOUR HORN! The only way the interviewer will know that you specialize in a certain area, that you have received awards, or that you were a ROCKSTAR at organizing a project, is if you tell them!

Invest in your strengths. I am no good at electrical engineering. I would not know the first thing about the industry. I am very good at coaching and training. Would it make more sense for me to spend 60% of my day trying to improve my knowledge base concerning electrical engineering, or delve into becoming a better coach and trainer? I hope the answer seems obvious. If you are a Human Resources professional, look into obtaining your certifications. If you are in the information technology field do the same. Make yourself as attractive as you possibly can for your next potential employer. Read industry publications. Attend seminars that focus on your field of interest.

Make your strengths so strong that they overpower your weaknesses.

If you feel that resume writing is not your best skill, hire a professional resume writer. Just make sure that you are well versed with the resume prepared for you and that it capitalizes on your strengths; those things that make you the best candidate for the job.

Step 6: **Educate Yourself**

I am an advocate of formal education, but that is not necessarily what I am referring to in this section. Although I mentioned previously that, you should not focus on your weaknesses; I do think you should do the homework required to position yourself for success. One of my clients, after having been employed with his organization for over a decade, disclosed to me that he has a difficult time putting spreadsheets together. He has never mastered basic computer software skills, and now that he has a new, very demanding manager, he is concerned that his job is in jeopardy.

Although it might seem like a longshot to apply for a promotion to become a medical doctor from the position of a nursing assistant, learning enough information about the team lead or office manager position is very realistic and doable if you are willing to put in the work.

In this day and age of technology, there is little excuse for "I don't know". Subscribe to RSS feeds (Rich Site Summary, often-dubbed Really Simple Syndication) to stay up to date on materials in the field you desire to move up in. The World Wide Web is bursting with details concerning just about everything! Google has been promoted to a verb in the English language. If you do not know how to do something, GOOGLE IT! Read blogs from experts in your field. Hit the library (or the Kindle store) and read books about the industry. Network with others from whom you can learn. Whatever you do, do not allow what you consider a lack of formal education to be your excuse for staying in your comfort zone.

Step 7: Develop a Plan

If one more job seeker says, they are 'applying for ANYTHING they can find on job search websites' I might scream! I am all for massive job search efforts in order to land your ideal position. This means lots of research and preparation. Not blindly sending out a bazillion resumes online to any company that happens to be hiring.

"A recent study ... reports that 61% cited networking as the source of their new jobs, while only 6% found jobs through Internet job sites and print ads. Therefore . . . spend time NETWORKING! *source: PR Newswire, 4/22/09

Instead – create a plan that will allow you to reach your job search goals. This may seem like an enormous undertaking to do on your own, but I assure you it is as easy as adding a few tasks to your current daily activities. If you are not sure what you want to do, search for assessments that will identify your skills, interests, values, or other traits. **Use your networks!** Join as many free organizations as you possibly can. You can make valuable contacts through your local chambers and other organizations where professionals hang out. **Attend support groups and job clubs in your area. Frequent job search training sessions or related training as a part of your overall job search plan.** You can meet new people while acquiring skills that can only benefit you in your new career.

Chat about it! Talk with people every day about your job search. Use your social media networks to let others know how they can help you. **Attend job fairs**, but do not just peruse the tables. Make a concerted effort to shake the hand and get the contact information of every potential employer in which you may be interested. Dropping off your resume in a box as you walk by each table is not a good use of your time. Make yourself memorable! The person you are talking to will see at least 100 people that day. How will you stand out?

Follow up! Even if you are not selected for a position, send a thank you note letting the recipient know that you would still be interested should the selected applicant not work out. Not many applicants do this, so at the very least you will be forefront in mind if their candidate falls through.

Step 8: Document - Document - DOCUMENT!

Because a job hunt can be a lengthy process, keep a diary of where you have applied and whether or not you have heard back. Although you do not think you will forget where you have applied, after a dozen applications, your memory can escape you. Sending more than one resume to the same employer says, "I'm disorganized and I don't care enough to keep up with the details of my own job search".

Remember, job hunting is a job in itself. If you do not manage your own work, how will you manage work for a company? It makes life so much easier when you have a paper trail detailing your job search efforts; it allows you to tell what is working and what is not. Maintaining a log can identify what changes you should make to your resume. If you have been passed over for

50 positions as an Administrative Assistant, it is possible that your resume is not selling hiring managers on your ability as such.

I had a client a couple of years ago who did an excellent job at chronicling his search efforts. He created a page in Microsoft Notes for each company he has applied. He kept a log of each contact made via phone and email, specifying names and titles of the person with whom he communicated. This made it easy to know what was going on at each company with which he applied. If he received notice that the position closed and he was not selected, he documented it so he did not inadvertently contact them again regarding that position.

Nothing seems more disorganized than a hiring manager calling to schedule an interview and having the applicant ask questions like, "which company is this again?" or "what position did I apply for there?" It sounds ludicrous, but it happens. Job seekers give the excuse, "I'm sorry, but I've applied at many places over the last few weeks". Make the hiring manager feel like their company is the company where you WANT to work. Keep good records.

I have included a job search diary that you can copy and use during your job search. *See appendix.*

Step 9: **Expect Success**

I heard one job seeker say, "I don't know if I'll get this job. I am not as experienced as some of the other candidates." If you are unsure about applying for a job — why would you apply? That sounds like a harsh question but, really; why? I mentioned earlier in this book the power of I AM statements. When you think a certain way about yourself, it will govern the way you speak about yourself.

You have the capacity to create circumstances with your words. Am I saying that just because you say — "I've got the job" you will have it? No. What I am saying however, is that your thoughts and your words will influence your attitude and behavior. When you feel extremely confident about an opportunity, the likelihood is that you will exude that confidence in your interview, and your post interview actions will be that of someone who expects success. You will not forget to call or write the interviewer to thank them for interviewing you. You will have childcare arranged, because you fully expect to have to start your new job very soon. You will have picked out your outfit for the first day of work in anticipation of that phone call offering you the job.

I once heard my pastor tell a story about a man who had his congregation pray for rain during a time of drought. They prayed in the morning and were instructed to come back in the evening for church service. When they assembled that night, the preacher seemed visibly upset. He told them to go home before preaching one word! When questioned why he seemed so disturbed, he answered: "You didn't believe! You had no expectation of rain!" When they disagreed, he proclaimed, "Where are your umbrellas?!"

Your belief or level of expectation will drive your actions. What are you expecting?

Step 10:

Know Employment Etiquette!

So, you've landed your ideal job. What things are imperative for you to know to maximize your time with this employer? Some of these things seem so 'common sense', however I have learned over the years never to assume that everyone knows how to conduct himself or herself on the job.

ଔ **Leave your cell phone off during working hours**

Your employer may not chastise you for using your cell phone on the job, but in my experience, silence does not mean approval. I have seen companies make decisions not to give greater responsibility, pay increases, or additional opportunities to a staff member who developed a habit of constantly talking on the phone or texting during work hours. Set yourself up for success. Leave personal conversations to personal time.

❧ **Remember that the customer is the reason you have your job**

Regardless of what type of job you have, you have a customer. You might think that only retail environments or service companies have customers, but if you work, you have a customer too. Some of your customers are internal, (the people you work with) others are external (the people who buy from you). Businesses fire people every day for improperly handling their customers. Branding, customer service, and image are all important to building customer loyalty. If you are repelling customers with a bad attitude or ignorance of your product or service, you become a liability to your organization. The next time you receive excellent customer service, remember how it makes you feel, and strive to give that feeling to ALL of your customers.

❧ Leave the workplace out of your social media rants

Let's just say your boss ticked you off today. How you handle that is a great indicator of your character. We all need a person in our life to whom we can vent. Key word: person. Using the World Wide Web as a venue for a rant session on social media is not going to advance your career. I have recently started developing social media policies for my clients. Employees using their Facebook profile and Twitter feeds as a way to stick it to their employer undercover precipitated this action. The problem with that is – it is not undercover. What you do online lasts forever, and the likelihood that you are connected to someone who is connected to someone who is connected to your boss is high. Do not jeopardize your job in a moment of online rage. Write it on paper instead. Get it all out of you, and then shred it in a cross-cut shredder. It will serve you better on paper than online.

☙ Understand and abide by workplace policies

If you are not clear on your employers expectations, the potential is great that you might not live up to your manager's hopes. Take time to inquire about policies and procedures. Read the orientation manual – you will be ahead of the pack because the average person will not read the policy manual in detail. Ask questions about items you do not understand. The worst that could happen is that you become the work place go to person relating to policies. If you look like the expert, you will surely be in good standing for promotion over those who do not know diddly about the company's requirements.

❧ Dress for where you are going not where you are

Earlier we discussed dressing in a way that is authentic to your personal style while maintaining a high level of professionalism. While this is extremely important, equally as imperative is deciding what you ultimately want to do in your career and acting "as if" now. Acting "as if" means literally seeing yourself in that role in the present.

No matter what you may think, managers often make hiring decisions that are influenced by the way a person dresses. Take a walk in the executive suite. If you aspire to be the next Vice President of Human Resources (or whatever you have your sights set on) examine how others in that role dress. You may just be the Human Resource Generalist or Executive Assistant right now, but coupled with professional development and being a great employee, dressing for success will be instrumental in getting you to that corner office on the top floor.

Do not let financial limitations keep you from dressing appropriately in order to snag that 'next level' role. Search out thrift stores. Find out the best resale boutiques (men and women) in your area. You would be surprised how easily you can locate name brand items at a fraction of the cost! I have a couple of friends who have very high powered positions, and make six figure salaries, but only shop in resale stores. They often boast about paying $10 or $12 dollars for what would normally be very expensive clothing items. No excuses! Just do it!

❧ Communicate professionally (written, verbal, listening, and responsiveness)

The way you articulate inspires confidence in your boss about your ability to lead and operate at peak performance. Spend time reading, take courses online (even YouTube!) practice your communication skills. During a meeting take notes, pay attention, and ask questions when unsure about what your supervisor wants. Listening is a large part of communication and it is essential to respond correctly to any request that has been made of you. I often give assignments to contractors, asking for assistance with presentations or reports for my clients. Some of the most time consuming errors made, could have been avoided, by listening and clarifying what was unclear. Your boss will appreciate your listening skills when you submit a report that has addressed every item to which he or she inquired.

Giving acknowledgement of receipt and providing a status is an important facet of communication. Many professionals are too busy to stop what they are doing to find out where you are on an assignment or to even verify that you received the email instructing you to begin. A simple reply stating this fact, along with periodic status reports will put your manager's mind at ease knowing that you are moving towards completion. Communicating your progress is another way to inspire faith in your boss when opportunities arise for greater responsibility and more money. If they know they can count on you; they should be happy to recommend you for promotion.

ল **Learn how to work with unlovely people**

This is probably one of the most important pieces of employment etiquette I can provide: In the world of work, you will inevitably encounter a coworker, supervisor, employee, or CEO who seems to be the bane of your existence. How will you remain the focused, productive, sane person that you must be, in order to keep your job and move forward in your career, in the face of this new-found antagonist? Take control. First, you must realize your control limits. You cannot change a jerk, so if the person you are dealing with is indeed a jerk, accept it. What you can control is your attitude and your response.

Check yourself – Make sure that you are not super sensitive to certain types of people. Yes, the person you work with might be offensive, but you also may be carrying baggage from a previous boss, old boyfriend or girlfriend, even a parent of whom co-worker reminds you. If this is the case, be aware and deal with the inward issues you may have.

Be the teacher – You teach people how to treat you every day. Do not allow someone to behave towards you in a manner that makes you uncomfortable. You must learn to professionally stand your ground without burning bridges or lowering yourself to the level of the offender. Although it may seem as though I am putting all of the responsibility on you, instead of the '*unlovely*', realize that YOU ultimately determine your position in most relationships. Do not forget that there is always a root cause for a person's behavior. Do not personalize the actions unless they are overtly (even subtly) abusive. If need be, go through the proper channels such as talking to your Human Resources Manager. Under no circumstances should you allow yourself to be baited into a situation that could cost you your job, respect from your peers, or even worse your safety. We will discuss this more in your next handbook, Empowered with Employment Etiquette.

I hope you are thinking, "Wow, that was simple. I can do this". You absolutely can do this. Do not allow this booklet to sit in your desk or under your bed. Use the resources here to chart your path to success. I made this small enough to fit in your purse, or maybe even your back pocket on purpose. I want you to remind yourself that not only can you secure a job you love; you can rock it! You are God's superstar. No one can do your job like you. Believe it! Act on it! Go get it!

I am ALWAYS here if you need me. -

Tish

To reach me visit www.TishTimes.com

About the author: Tish Times, founder and CEO of HireTimes Career & Coaching Group, has worked for over seventeen years in the employment industry both as an employee and a business owner. She excels at empowering job seekers so they can optimize their job search and capitalize on their strengths in order to become more attractive to potential employers. Tish assists employees in branding themselves for career growth or embarking upon a new career path. Tish specializes in helping companies increase employee engagement, create a harmonious work environment, and ensure compliance with federal employment laws. Tish is a staff coach who concentrates on human resource issues and management development to create forward thinking workplaces. Tish is also a professional facilitator, speaker, and trainer. She is a frequent speaker for professional associations and conferences regarding employment, work performance, customer service, anti-harassment, confidence building, assertiveness in the workplace and a host of other life issues. Because of Times' expertise and skill, her workshops, one-to-one consultations, group facilitations, and individual performance coaching are not the typical "packaged" programs. Her ability to address free-flowing dialogue and inquiry allows individuals and groups to grow past their own obstacles and develop tools for success.

Tish has a national base of individual and organizational clients. Prior to starting HireTimes Career & Coaching Group, Tish owned a temporary staffing company and managed a non-profit organization.

Most recently, Tish has developed the Passionate Career Academy, a group coaching program for people seeking to jump-start their career searches or improve their career paths. She has also created Unlock Your AMAZING! ™ , a holistic group coaching program designed to help participants land their dream job, attract more ideal clients, and/or have more rewarding relationships.

She presents highly interactive workshops in both live and virtual formats. Tish hosts a weekly internet radio program called **Loving Work & Growing Business with Tish Times** on www.blogtalkradio/tishtimes. She also facilitates a monthly event called the **HireTimes Networking Event** created to provide an environment for hiring managers and job seekers to connect in a comfortable setting over lunch. For more information on her expertise and services, go to **www.hiretimescg.com**. To have Tish Times as a speaker for your next event, hire her as your career or business coach, or subscribe to The Passionate Career Blog visit **www.tishtimes.com** or contact her at **tishtimes@hiretimescg.com**

Appendix

Tips for Creating a Great Resume

Landing a job is not the purpose of the resume; rather, its purpose is to help you obtain a job interview.

> ➤ A resume is a marketing tool — an advertisement that highlights your education, skills, qualifications, and experiences.
>
> ➤ It should arouse an employer's interest and motivate the employer to contact you for more information.
>
> ➤ Think of your resume as a **dynamic and constantly changing** document. Format and target your resume(s) to market your best qualifications for specific jobs.

- ➤ **Lead with your strengths.** Put first the parts of your education, experience, and skills that will be of greatest interest to the employer. Make them the most detailed and prominent part of your resume. Make it easy for an employer to see that you are a qualified candidate who should be invited for an interview.

- ➤ Determine the purpose of each resume and address that purpose. For example, if you are applying for a marketing position, focus on your marketing experience.

- ➤ A resume's brevity emphasizes the importance of the information you select to include. Write in a straightforward style and do not repeat information.

- ➤ Resumes must be typographically and grammatically perfect, honest and verifiable, targeted and results oriented. Proofread! Spell check does not catch proper names and homophones/homonyms.

- ➤ Some employers scan resumes to determine qualifications. Include industry- or occupation-specific keywords as they relate to your skills and experience

Types of Resumes:

1. Chronological: The chronological resume is the most widely used resume and is preferred by many employers. The educational and work experience is presented in reverse chronological sequence (current or most recent first) with short, concise statements about each work experience.

2. Functional: This style suits individuals making a career change, re-entering the workplace, or those who have frequently changed jobs. It emphasizes skills and qualifications developed in work and draws upon work experience, education, and personal background. Headings are used to separate particular skills. Sample headings include: "Managerial Skills," "Financial Skills," and "Organizational Skills."

3. Combination: The combination resume is a blend of chronological and functional. Less traditional headings may be used while maintaining basic chronological format.

4. Artistic Fields: You may demonstrate your creative or artistic skills by using a less traditional layout and font style, but prepare a traditional resume to accompany your creative resume.

Should the resume be one page or two?

If you are a current student or recent graduate, you may be able to fit your resume on one page. However, do not short-change yourself by omitting significant information just for the sake of a one-page resume. Keep the information focused on your qualifications, skills and accomplishments.

If you do go onto a second page be certain that the second page is as strong as the first, and fill at least ⅓ of the second page. If you do add a second page, type your name, "page two of two," and your phone number in the top right or top left corner; this way, if the first page becomes separated from the second, an employer will be able to contact you. Limit your resume to two pages.

Should I list references on my resume?

List references on a separate page. You do not need to type the phrase, "references available upon request" on your resume. If an employer wants to see references, the employer will ask you for them.

Should I just use a template?

Templates, such as those found in Microsoft Word, can limit your flexibility. They can be rigid or hard to reformat and may not be your most effective way to showcase your skills. Avoid the "cookie cutter" look. Create a distinctly personal impression by designing your own resume.

What if I have no relevant experience?

If you have had numerous jobs throughout college you do not need to list every job, especially if it's not related to the position to which you are applying. You should list all related jobs. If your related and unrelated jobs are out of order sequentially you can include a section entitled "Related Experience" and another one entitled "Other Work Experience." This allows employers to see your related jobs first, rather than including your unrelated and related jobs together.

What sections should my resume have?

Each resume consists of sections that group your experiences together in a meaningful way. The following slides will show examples of sections that your resume may/may not contain. Some resume sections may not apply to you.

> Organize your information using headings that will help you highlight your strengths *as they relate to the desired job*.

> Arrange sections in an order that best markets your skills and experience.

> Lead with your strengths. Put first and make most detailed and prominent the parts of your education, experience and skills that will be of greatest interest to the employer.

> Make it easy for an employer to see that you are a qualified candidate who should be invited for an interview.

Heading:

This section includes:

> Your name (no non-professional nickname)

> Mailing address

- ➢ Phone number
- ➢ And email address

Be sure to include area and zip codes. All of this information is located at the top of the page and is typically centered.

- ➢ Use both current and permanent address when in transition
- ➢ Use one phone number per address where a reliable message can be left
- ➢ Use only a professional email address that you check regularly (you can set your professional or school email to forward to your personal account)
- ➢ Remember, your email address or voice message influences the impression a prospective employer develops of you. Be prepared to create a positive impression at any time.
- ➢ Do not include personal information such as sex, age, marital status, health or social security number.

Objective:

- ➢ Write an employer-centered objective that targets a specific job, employer and/or industry. Focus on what you can contribute to the company (such as the skills you can offer).

➢ The objective should be specific and it may change for each position you seek. Avoid using generic or trite phrases such as "an entry level position."

➢ If you include an objective, everything else on your resume should support or show evidence that you qualify for the targeted job.

➢ When posting your resume to a job search Web site, incorporate keywords in your objective that reflect your skills and career goals.

Summary/Profile:

➢ A profile highlights the best of your qualifications for a particular job.

➢ You may use headings such as, "Profile," "Highlights," or "Summary of Qualifications."

➢ A well-written profile or summary can positively influence the way the rest of your resume is interpreted.

➢ It should address the all-important question on the hirer's mind, "What can this candidate do for the organization?" Select details that highlight your strengths.

- ➢ Statements in this section must be supported elsewhere in your resume. As a marketing statement, the profile may include the following kinds of information:

- ➢ "Hook" line - determine the essence of the job, then make a connection between what the employer needs and what you can do for the organization; convince employers that it is worth their time to continue to read your resume!

- ➢ Professional certifications

- ➢ Honors, awards, scholarships, any recognition you have received as a student, intern, employee, consultant, board member or volunteer; any published writing

- ➢ Any unique skills, e.g. fluency or conversational ability in a second language

- ➢ Statements in this section must be supported elsewhere in your resume. As a marketing statement, the profile may include the following kinds of information:

- ➢ Leadership roles or memberships in student clubs, sports, organizations; memberships in professional organizations or associations

➢ Technology skills and/or specialized equipment you can operate

➢ Transferable skills such as leadership, team work, customer service, problem solving

➢ Anything that speaks to your success!

TIP: If you feel it would be more effective to emphasize detail such as awards, skills or organization involvement, then consider listing such details in a separate section with its own heading rather than use a profile.

➢ For example, if your technical skills are your strongest qualification for a job, consider a separate section called "Technical Skills."

Education Section:

➢ List degrees or certifications, in reverse chronological order, current or most recent first, then list your major along with any minors or concentrations.

> ➢ Indicate the month and year when you graduated or expect to graduate. There is no need to include the words "expected" or "anticipated" before the month and year of graduation. On the next line list the name of the school, along with location (city, state).

> ➢ Recent grads may include coursework, but be sure it is unique and/or relates to the job. Do not list "Intro" or "Principles" courses.

> TIP: If you feel your experience is a greater strength and that employers will be more interested in your experience, then list "Experience" here and follow it with "Education" – lead with your strengths!

Experience Section:

You may use separate headings called "Related Experience" or "Other Experience" in order to highlight and put first your career-related experience. You also may include subheadings such as "Student Teaching Experience" and "Research Experience."

Do not minimize the value of food service, retail and other college work experience. Employers want to know that you know how to treat customers, how to get along with co-workers, how to communicate effectively and work as a team member, and how to respond to supervision.

Using key words of your field focus on the skills and tasks developed at each job. Write in short concise statements using action verbs and adjectives to describe each skill or task. Cite specific responsibilities and accomplishments for each position. Statements may be displayed in either bullet or paragraph style.

TIP: Avoid phrases such as "responsible for" and "duties include."

 ➢ Include your job title, name of organization, location (city,

state), and dates of employment (month/year).

 ➢ Show advancement in level of responsibility.

 ➢ Quantify information when appropriate and when the numbers are significant.

 ➢ Include any achievements, recognition, contributions, innovations, positive outcomes, anything that "works better" as a result of your being in the job or demonstrates your effectiveness.

Things to avoid in your objective:

- Do not use the personal pronouns like "I", "me", "mine", etc. in your resume. This will overshadow your information.

- Do not exceed your job objective more than three lines. Writing your job objective for more than the maximum limit will lower down the quality of your resume.

- Make use of job related keywords and phrases in your objective to present your desired skills. However, over using these keywords and action verbs will not help you. More number of keywords and phrases in your resume will make your resume sound ineffective.

More tips...

- Do not provide vague information in your resume. Be specific in describing the details of the position you are desiring and the knowledge you are seeking.

- Avoid simple grammatical and spelling mistakes in resume. Proof read the resume before taking the final print-out of it. Proof-reading the resume will help you to detect the errors occurred during your resume writing.

- Avoid using job objectives from sample resumes. Build your own resume objective and do not copy the objectives from samples.

- Avoid irrelevant information in your resume. Do not include the details that are not related to your applied position.
- Avoids negative words like hate, dislike and unhappy.
- Do not present incomplete information in your resume.
- Choose the proper format for your job objective. Do not use the resume format blindly. Use the format that best suits your details and highlights your qualities in best way.

Basics for using Social Media for Job Search:

What do I say?

⊙ **Status Update** - Post status updates relating to your job search, to keep it top of mind that you are still looking for a job. Say things like "I had a great interview this morning... keep your fingers crossed!" or "I have a networking meeting later today with a company I'm really interested in!"

- **Using LinkedIn** - Company Search - One of the best ways to use LinkedIn is if you have a very specific company you are interested in. You search on that company, and hopefully find people who are connected to other people you know. Then, you can ask your personal contact to connect you. Or, if you their monthly fee, you have the opportunity to email people who you don't have a contact in common with.

- LinkedIn allows employers to post jobs on the site. The jobs are usually high quality, professional jobs.

- **Email** - You can send an email to everyone in your LinkedIn network, letting him or her know of your situation, and asking for any help.

Tweet Tweet!

- The best part of <u>Twitter</u> is that it allows you to connect with people you do not know, based on common interests. What a great way to do networking!

- **Basic Networking** People (myself included) tweet about jobs all of the time! You can find out about open positions that will never be posted otherwise.

- ◉ Do not be afraid to connect with people you do not personally know.

- ◉ Pay attention to posts regarding job openings – and respond!

- ◉ Be aware of posts that give information about your potential employer's personality.

Blog!

- • The traditional way of searching for a job was proactive, forcing you to start a job that you might not have enjoyed. The new approach is about building a powerful personal brand and attracting job opportunities directly into your doorstep. How do you do this? You become a content producer instead of just a consumer and the number one way to do that on the web is to launch a blog that centers around both your expertise and passions.

You Tube:

- Many video resumes are good, while others are so amateur and rehearsed that they subtract from a given candidates marketing program. The key with a video resume is that very few people have actually created one, so they serve as a differentiator in the recruiting process.

Develop Early Work-Life Balance

- Build downtime into your schedule
  - > When searching for your ideal position, take into consideration how the workload will affect your home life; family and energy
- Drop activities that sap your time or energy
  - > Look at your overall life. Realize that your life may change once you start your new career. Determine what you may want to decrease or drop altogether.

Maximize Productivity on the Job

- **Take a break.**
- **Set a timer** for each of your tasks.
- **Eliminate all distractions.** This includes the phone, email notifications, and having multiple web browsers open on the desktop.

- **Distractions should be avoided, but sometimes a bit of music in the background can help you focus.** Of course, it does not need to be heavy rock music, but a bit of Beethoven may do you some good.

- **Love what you do.** Enjoying what you do is the ultimate way to increase your productivity.

- **Complete your most dreaded tasks first thing in the morning.** Whichever activity you are dreading the most is probably the one you need to complete first thing in the morning.

- **Just start.** Often times, starting is the hardest part. Once you get going, you will quickly get into a rhythm that could last for hours.

- **Keep a notebook and pen on hand at all times.** This way, you can write down your thoughts, to-dos, and ideas at any time. The key is to get everything out of your head and onto paper. This way, your subconscious mind will not be reminding you about it every other second.

- **Write a blog to chronicle your own personal development and achievements.** This keeps you accountable and always working towards self-improvement and personal growth.

- **Step away from the computer.** The Internet has become one of the number one distractions. To increase your productivity, try to do as much of your work offline as possible.
- **Write out a to-list each day.**

When starting your new job:

- Give Yourself 90 Days
- Build the New Skills You Need
- Navigate the New Culture
- Learn Who's Who
- Make sure you understand from your first day why you were hired and what your goals are for the first 6–12 months. This can help with your direction in the weeks to come.
- It is not weak to ask for help. If you do not know how or where to find the information you need, you'll waste your time if you search for it yourself. Ask your boss or colleagues for help when you need it.
- Many people feel overwhelmed when they start with a new company. Everything is dramatically different, which can leave you feeling stressed and chaotic.

- ◉ Avoid making comparisons between your new company and your old company. Your new team does not want to hear "At my old job, we used to..." Focus on what you need to do now, not what or how you did something in the past.

- ◉ If someone on your new team does not respond well to you, do not take it personally – at least in the beginning. Remember, you might be in a role that someone else used to have, and that person might have been a friend of this team member. It will take time to establish trust.

- ◉ Do not allow yourself to be caught up in the copycat game. In the workplace and in the marketplace authenticity reigns! Even if you are not initially popular, you will always be respected.

Amazing ME! – write five things that are AMAZING about you!

1.
2.

3.	
4.	
5.	

I AM Statements Template

Fill in the blank

1. I AM	
2. I AM	
3. I AM	
4. I AM	
5. I AM	
6. I AM	

7. I AM	
8. I AM	
9. I AM	
I AM	

Create a Job Search Diary in MS Excel similar to this to keep up with positions you have applied for

Job Search Diary:				
Date	Company	Contact name or email	Position Applied for	Notes

Job Clubs and Networking Organizations I Need to Research:

∾ 60% of all jobs are found via networking

-   Use networking as a part of your overall job search strategy

-   Make a great impression
  - o   Write your target organizations here:

Employers make judgments about you based on the questions you ask. Have you done your homework on the organization? Are you asking shallow questions that you could find in a web search, but about which you have no interest? Are you asking about salary? **DON'T!!** Are your questions intelligent and thoughtful and cordial?

Sample Questions to Ask the Interviewer:

- What are the organization's/company's strengths and weaknesses compared to its competition?

- How does upper management view the role and importance of this department and this position?

- What is the organization's plan for the next five years, and how does this department fit in?

- Could you explain your organizational structure?

- What do you most enjoy about your work with this organization / company / agency?

- What type of training is provided for this position?

- What are the various ways employees communicate with one another to carry out their work?

- How will my leadership responsibilities and performance be measured? By whom?

- What are the day-to-day responsibilities of this job?

Recommended Reading List:

Beyond Ordinary by Dr. Mikel Brown

Dare To Discover Yourself by Gary N. Sparkman

<u>Help! My Boss is an Idiot. The Training Manual for the Uninspired Employee</u> by Michael Yeary, MBA

<u>Brand Me. Make Your Mark: Turn Passion into Profit</u> by Melissa Dawn Johnson

<u>Job Searching with Social Media for Dummies</u> by Joshua Waldman

www.ingramcontent.com/pod-product-compliance
Lightning Source LLC
Chambersburg PA
CBHW041529090426
42738CB00035B/13